ST. CHRISTOPHERS

for General

THE STORY OF THE
POST

ROBERT PAGE

ADAM & CHARLES BLACK : LONDON

BLACK'S JUNIOR REFERENCE BOOKS
General Editor: R. J. Unstead

This book is printed in Baskerville 14 pt.
with headings in Mercurius Bold Script

© 1967 A. AND C. BLACK LTD

FIRST PUBLISHED 1967
BY A. AND C. BLACK LTD
4, 5 AND 6 SOHO SQUARE, LONDON, W.1

MADE AND PRINTED IN GREAT BRITAIN
BY MORRISON AND GIBB LTD
LONDON AND EDINBURGH

CONTENTS

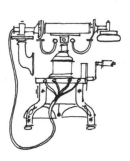

Acknowledgements

The drawings in this book are by Denis Wrigley.

Grateful acknowledgement is also made to the following for permission to reproduce photographs and drawings:

H. M. Postmaster General, 18, 19a, 20a, 22, 27a, 28, 29a and b, 30, 32, 34, 36a, 37b, 40a and b, 42a, 43b, 48, 49b, 53, 54a and b, 57, 58, 59a and b, 60a and b, 61b, 62, 63.

Illustrated London News, 36b, 38a.

The residuary legatees of the estate of the late C. F. Dendy-Marshall, 16a, 38b.

Radio Times Hulton Picture Library, 12b, 31a.

Grateful acknowledgement is also made to various contributors to *Postscript*—the journal of the Society of Postal Historians.

Several of the photographs are of items in the author's collection.

COURIER ANGLOIS

1 SOME EARLY POSTS

"In the name of King Ahasuerus was it written and sealed with the King's ring. And the letters were sent by posts into all the King's provinces. The posts went out, being hastened by the King's commandment."

"So the posts that rode upon mules and camels (and young dromedaries) went out, being hastened and pressed on by the King's commandment."

These words come from the Old Testament, from chapters 3 and 8 of the Book of Esther. King Ahasuerus, also called Xerxes, was king of Persia about 2,500 years ago. As lord of an empire that stretched from "India unto Ethiopia", he often wanted to send letters to the governors of his various provinces.

To do this, he kept a number of messengers called *posts* who carried the king's letters with all possible speed. A famous Greek historian, named Herodotus, praised this Persian system. The king's letters, he said, were carried very quickly and very regularly.

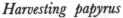

Harvesting papyrus

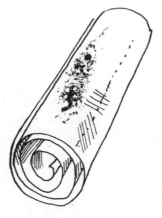

A papyrus roll

Cuneiform writing

The Egyptians used writing material made from papyrus, a reed which grew by the river. Letters might also be written on clay tablets, using cuneiform script

In Ancient Egypt, postal systems were set up as early as 2000 B.C., for a father writing to his son at about that date mentions "the post leaving for abroad". Letters have been found which were written by the rulers of the Hittites, Babylon, Cyprus and other countries of the Middle East, between the years 1400 and 1350 B.C. All these were royal letters; private letters were not carried.

In 550 B.C. Cyrus the Great, King of Persia, set up a postal system in his own country and later extended it to the countries he had conquered: Babylon, Media, Assyria, Arabia and other parts of Asia Minor. Herodotus wrote of these posts that "neither rain nor snow prevented them from carrying out their appointed task". These words are now engraved over the entrance to the Head Post Office in New York.

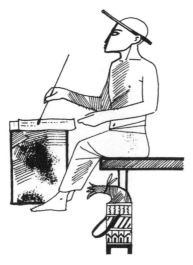

An Egyptian scribe

About 320 B.C. the Egyptians set up their own internal post. An internal post is one which deals with letters to be delivered to towns and villages of the country in which they are written. So many letters were written that there was a twice-daily service between the Court at Thebes and Upper Egypt.

This service was well planned and records were kept by the Postmaster of Fayoum. These show that the "office" at Fayoum handled the letters to and from Upper Egypt. The times of arrival and sending out of letters, together with the actual names of the couriers, were also noted.

An Egyptian river boat

Another document of the same period stated that the postmaster had 44 couriers or messengers, and that there was a separate camel service for parcels. To make this service safer, police guards travelled with the messengers. At the same time there was a boat service on the river Nile, but this was much slower and was used by the public.

A few years before the birth of Jesus, Egypt was conquered by the Romans who, as always, set the defeated people to work to build better roads. Travel became swifter and the postal service improved. In Egypt, as well as in other countries in the Roman Empire, a kind of general post, called Cursus Publicus, was set up. The mail was carried by messengers on horseback, or in horse carts, through a series of relay stations called "mutationes". At each of these stations fresh teams of horses were kept in readiness.

About A.D. 300 one of the officials of the Roman post in Egypt was named Maximian. To make sure that the local postmasters in the relay stations were doing their work properly, Maximian appointed a number of inspectors.

The Romans also introduced two parcel posts, one being an express service and the other a slower general post.

A Roman horse cart

2 PIGEON POSTS AND OTHER POSTS OF THE MIDDLE AGES

Another postal system of early times was set up by the Arabs. In A.D. 679 Khalif Moawia began the Arab posts, and although he died in the next year, his successor, Khalif Yazid, continued the work. From Baghdad there radiated, like the spokes of a great wheel, six postal roads to the distant parts of the Arab kingdom. On these six roads there were no less than 959 relay stations, roughly thirteen miles (or one day's journey) apart. There were two kinds of post: a fast one for which horses were used, and a slower one for which camels and foot messengers were used.

In A.D. 1250 the Mamelukes became the most powerful people in Egypt and the Middle East. Their power lasted until 1517. These people brought several new ideas into the postal services. They gave the couriers a uniform, which consisted of a yellow silk scarf bearing a large silver badge. On one side of this badge there was the confession of faith from the Koran, the holy book of Mohammed the Prophet, and on the other side was the name of the Sultan. They also improved and enlarged the existing pigeon post.

A Mameluke

Pigeons had been used before to carry messages. The ancient Greeks used them to send the results of the Olympic games to the various towns in Greece. The Romans used them as early as 43 B.C. and the Chinese had pigeon posts in A.D. 673. Arab pigeon posts were started in Arabia in the eighth century, but they were not introduced into Egypt until A.D. 1146. The Mamelukes set up pigeon lofts every seven miles along each postal route.

Blue pigeons were used for this general service, but there was an "express" service in which racing birds were used.

Strict rules were laid down about the type of message which could be sent. All unnecessary words had to be left out in much the same way as a telegram is written today. Only thin paper could be used, and the sheets were small in size. Paper as we know it was in general use by the ninth century, and Arab paper was made chiefly from linen.

It was usual to send each letter twice by different birds as there was always the danger of pigeons being killed by hawks.

An English pigeon-cote of the Middle Ages

Huge numbers of birds were kept and it is estimated that at the end of the thirteenth century there were nearly two thousand birds in the lofts at Cairo alone. At the beginning of the sixteenth century the Arab lands were captured by the Turks and the pigeon post ended.

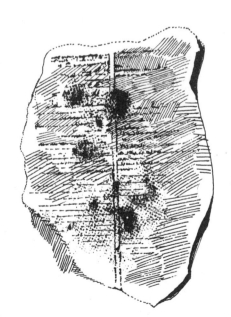

Some letters were written on clay tablets

In this short chapter only a few of the early posts of the world have been mentioned, but enough to show that postal services arose when kings and military governors needed to write to one another. As knowledge of writing increased, merchants and private persons began sending letters.

Not all letters were carried by the posts. Some were delivered "by hand". This means that they were delivered by friends or servants of the writers, especially when the distances were short. Old letters of this type, sometimes called "bearer letters", can be seen in museums. Some of them were written on clay tablets. One such letter, written in 2000 B.C. in the city of Nineveh, is from one merchant to another complaining that some goods he had ordered had not been sent.

In Europe in the Middle Ages four main types of post grew up. The *Royal Post* for carrying Court messages and State documents was the oldest. The second was the *Monastic Post*. A large number of the learned men of those times lived in monasteries and a service, started by the monks themselves, carried letters between the various monasteries.

The third, perhaps the most important of all, was the *Merchant Post*. The large number of letters which have been found written by Venetian and other merchants in the thirteenth, fourteenth and fifteenth centuries show that there was a very large and well-run postal system. The fourth type was the *Judicial Post* dealing with matters of law. It was used by judges and lawyers. In time these separate systems merged into the single postal service we have today.

This letter was sent from Beyrouth to Tripoli in 1506. The message was written on one side of the sheet of paper and then the letter was folded, addressed and sealed. You can see the sealing wax and some of the original sealing silk which was used to tie it

The Merchant Post was carried in ships such as these

Few of the early kings of England were interested in reading and writing. They left the writing of their letters to their scribes and then "signed" them with sealing wax and a signet ring. But one of the early Norman kings, Henry I, known as Henry Beauclerk or "good scholar", was interested in letter writing. He considered that the delivery of his letters was an important matter, so he employed carriers whom he called *Nuncii* or *Cursores*. They were chosen for their honesty, bravery and fitness. Obviously it was no easy task to be a carrier of the king's despatches.

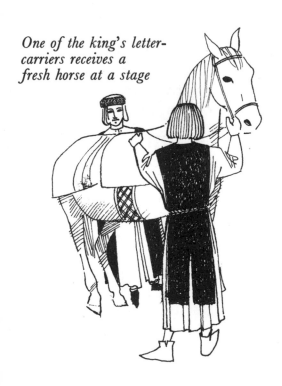

One of the king's letter-carriers receives a fresh horse at a stage

Henry III fitted out his carriers in livery or uniform and Edward I set up fixed stages where horses were kept in readiness for the Nuncii so that they should not be delayed in their journeys. In old account books there are many references to money being paid to those men. For example, in the Black Prince's register of 1359 are these entries: "£10 paid to Edward the messenger" and "40/- paid to Thomas the messenger". Urgent letters sometimes bore special instructions such as "Haste, Post, Haste —For thy life". Others carried drawings of gallows as a warning lest the messenger should loiter on the way.

In 1482, Henry IV began the *postboy system*. The roads were so bad that the king gave orders that good horses were to be kept at inns or "stages" about twenty miles apart. Thus, his postboys could obtain fresh horses and they were given permission to ride off the roads through private land and even through crops if necessary. Naturally, the post became unpopular with farmers and landowners.

By Tudor times, the need for a regular postal service was growing. New lands had been discovered, trade was increasing, kings made alliances, quarrelled with each other and borrowed money for their wars from the rich Italian city states.

Sir Brian Tuke, Henry VIII's Master of the Post

Merchants in Hamburg and Venice did business with merchants in London and Southampton. Books were being printed, gold was arriving from the New World and spies were at work in every capital of Europe. All this activity meant that more letters were written and had to be delivered.

In 1517, Henry VIII made Sir Brian Tuke the Master of the King's Post and paid him a yearly salary of £66 13s. 4d. (This does not sound very much, but the pound was worth many times more than it is today.) Sir Brian found many difficulties. The postboys were no longer honest and brave like the Nuncii, and the horse stage system at the posthouses was badly managed. The horses meant for the postboys were often hired out to farmers or travellers.

Many parts of the country were not served by these posthouses, so the post-boys were granted the right, when in these areas, to demand private mounts from the ordinary townsfolk.

These posts were mainly royal posts; few private letters were carried. If they were, the postmaster had the right to open and read them. This was a kind of censorship, or security check, such as is carried out in war-time.

4 ELIZABETHAN POSTS

When Elizabeth I became Queen, many more people were learning to read and write, but so far there was no official post to carry private letters. Writers of private letters had to rely on the public carrier.

The public carrier was very important to both the townsfolk and the villagers. In his great lumbering waggon, often drawn by four or more horses, he carried parcels and letters between the villages and towns. He was always welcome, because he was also the carrier of news and gossip, which he passed on—not always accurately. But because of the bad roads and his heavy waggon, he was a very slow traveller, averaging 120 miles in eight days—about $1\frac{1}{2}$ miles per hour! Some carriers, who could afford to pay helpers, often rode ahead, on horseback, with letters and light parcels, so as to speed up delivery.

The public carrier

Two proclamations concerning the post were issued in 1583. The first one was a royal proclamation which said quite definitely that no private mail was to be carried. The postboy was to ride at seven miles an hour in summer and not less than five miles an hour in winter. He had to blow his horn at least three times each mile, and was to carry two leather bags lined with baize.

The second proclamation was made by the Chief Postmaster, Thomas Randolph. He knew that more people wanted to send letters by post, so he stated that he did not mind private letters being carried by the Queen's post as long as Her Majesty's packets were delivered first.

The postboy had to blow his horn at least three times each mile

A postmaster awaits the arrival of the post with horses already harnessed

In 1603 two separate kinds of post came into being, the Packet Post and the Thorough (or Through) Post. The first was the royal post and for this each postmaster was told to keep at least two horses ready harnessed. When he received a postal packet he was to send it on within fifteen minutes to the next stage, after entering all details in a book. He was also to write on each letter the time when each messenger arrived. He was to have ready two leather bags lined with baize or cotton to hold the letters. He was also to provide messengers with horns which were to be blown at least four times in each mile.

Private letters were to be sent by the new Through Post. In this post the letters were to be carried the whole distance by one messenger who could change horses at the stages. He had to pay for them, in advance, at 2½d. a mile. In the Packet Post both messengers and horses changed at the stages. Postboys were made to carry warrants which they had to show before they could claim fresh post horses.

5 ORGANISING AND ESTABLISHING THE POSTAL SYSTEM

In the year 1635 Charles I issued a proclamation about the post. On the 31st of July of that year the Packet Post or Crown Post which was costing the king about £3,400 a year was made a public post. This meant that ordinary folk could send letters at a fixed charge called the postal rate, and have them delivered to the post towns.

At this time the king, who was trying to rule the country without the help of Parliament, was getting short of money. So perhaps he was glad to rid himself of the cost of the royal post. A man named Thomas Witherings was made Chief Postmaster of England and he seems to have been a clever man, for he soon set up a full system of posts for the public to use along the six main post roads of the country. These six roads are still in use today: London to Edinburgh, London to Yarmouth, London to Dover, London to Plymouth, London to Bristol and London to Chester.

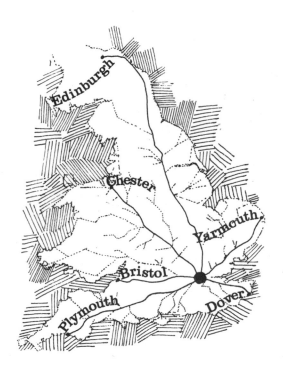

A map of Thomas Witherings's postal system. The black lines radiating from London show the six main post roads and the dotted lines show branch roads which were used for the post

*A token from Compton, near Guildford,
showing a postboy of about 1650*

Of course the postboys had to be paid and the people who wrote or received the letters had to provide the money. So the Chief Postmaster agreed to pay the postboys 3d. per mile, and to make a charge of 2d. up to 80 miles for a single letter (that is one written on a single sheet of paper), and up to 8d. to Scotland.

Before 1635 most private letters and light parcels had been carried by friends, messengers or the public carrier. Witherings knew that he could not do away with the old ways all at once. It has already been mentioned that carriers often rode on ahead of their lumbering waggons to deliver letters. To check this unofficial delivery of letters an order was made which said that no carrier was to be more than eight hours ahead or behind his own waggon. As the waggons travelled about fifteen miles a day, this order made sure that the carriers could only be short distances from their waggons. This had the effect of slowing up the carrier delivery and Witherings hoped that people would learn to use the quicker official post.

The attack on postboy Hickes

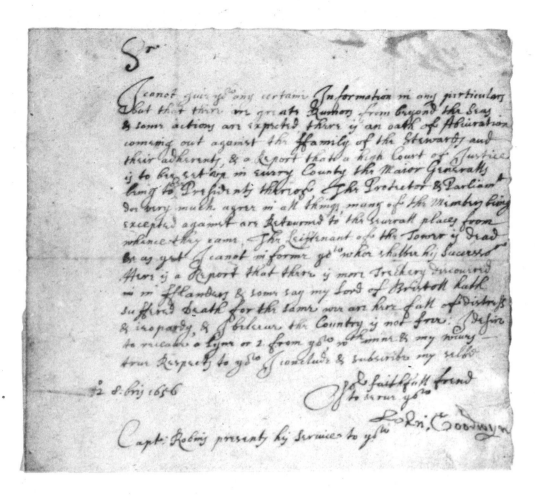

This letter of 1656 *names the letter-carrier—"Capt. Robins presents his services to you"*

When the Civil War broke out in 1642, Witherings was dismissed from his post as Chief Postmaster. A curious struggle then took place between the king, the House of Lords and the House of Commons as to who should control this new public post. On one occasion, a postboy named Hickes, who was carrying the Chester mail from Ireland, was attacked at Barnet by some supporters of the House of Lords.

It seems that they were successful in stealing the mail but at Highgate they themselves were attacked by five persons "on great horses, with pistols, habited (dressed) like troopers". These five men were friends of a man named Edmond Prideaux who had been chosen as the new Chief Postmaster by the House of Commons. There were several incidents like this but in the end the Commons or Parliamentary party won.

The title page of the first Post Office Act of 1657

When the Civil War was over and Oliver Cromwell was made Lord Protector, the first Post Office Act of Parliament was passed. It was called "An Act for the Setling of the Postage of England, Scotland and Ireland". It stated that there should be one General Post Office and one Postmaster General. This very important Act of 1657 set up, by law, a postal system which could be used by all people.

The office of Postmaster General was purchased from the government by the person who offered most money for it, providing that he was a suitable person. This method was called "farming". The person who took the office did it to make a living and before he could do so, he had to get back the money he had already paid.

Thus, he had to make sure that all letters were properly paid for and that all the money was handed in by the postboys. He had also to try to make the public use the official post, and to do this he tried to stop any "private" posts.

6 THE LATER STUART POSTS

Charles II returned to the throne in 1660 and the first Postmaster General of the new reign was a man from Sussex named Henry Bishop. Because more letters were being written and because there was more chance of making money out of managing the post, Henry Bishop had to pay a very large sum of money as the "farmer"—£21,500 each year.

The Postmaster General knew how important it was to him to keep a check on all letters going through the post, so he invented the first stamp. This was not what we call a stamp today. Henry Bishop's stamp was made by striking the letters with a handstamp, much the same as a postmaster today uses when he marks postal orders with a date stamp.

The Bishop Mark, as it is now known, was small and circular in shape. You can see it on the letter shown below.

Henry Bishop, Master of the Posts from 1660–1663

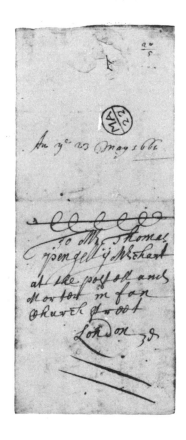

This letter shows an early Bishop Mark of 22nd May 1661

In the top half of the stamp was the month and in the lower half was the day of the month. There was no mark to show the year so it is impossible to know in which year a letter was written unless the writer happened to have dated it himself.

The month mark is always in a shortened form, consisting only of two letters: JA for January, FE for February, MR for March, AP for April, MA for May, etc.

An example of a Bishop Mark for 19th November

As in Witherings' time, the six post roads were used. There were no cross roads linking up these six roads. So if a letter was sent from York (which was on the Edinburgh road) to Manchester (served by the Chester road) it had to travel down the Edinburgh road to London, a distance of 196 miles, and then back up the Chester road to Manchester, a further 184 miles. This made a total distance of 380 miles. Had it been possible to send direct from York to Manchester, the letter would have had to travel only 64 miles.

A postboy of 1670

*One of Dockwra's placards
is torn down*

Up to this time, no arrangements had been made for the delivery of letters to private houses. They had to be collected from the receiving houses. Merchants often found that they had not time to do this, so many of them used private messengers.

One man, William Dockwra, thought there was a need for a properly arranged local post in London. So, on April 1st, 1680, he began his Penny Post for the City of London.

At first he met with a great deal of opposition. His placards were torn down by the city porters and by private messengers because they felt he was doing them out of their employment.

This is the first page of the pamphlet issued by William Dockwra to explain his system of a Penny Post. It was printed in 1681

The Practical Method

OF THE

PENNY-POST:

Being a Sheet very neceſſary for all Perſons to have by them,

For their Information in the Regular Uſe of a De-
ſign ſo well Approved of, for quickening Corre-
ſpondence, Promoting Trade and Publick Good.

*With an Explaination of the following Stamps, for the
Marking of all Letters.*

Hereas *William Dockwra* of *London* Merchant, and the reſt of the Undertakers, (who are all Natives and free Citizens of *London*) out of a ſence of the great benefit which would accrew to the nu-merous Inhabitants of this Great City, and adjacent parts, (with hopes of ſome Reaſonable Encouragement hereafter to Them-ſelves) have lately ſet up a *New Invention* to convey Letters and Parcels, not exceeding One Pound Weight, and Ten Pounds in Value, to and from all Parts within the Contiguous Buildings of the Weekly Bills Mortality for a Penny a Letter or Parcel, where-by Correſpondency, the Life of Trade and Buſineſs, is and will be much facilitated ; and having for above a year paſt, with great pains, and at ſome Thouſands of Pounds Charge, reduced the ſame into Practice, which does manifeſtly appear to be for the Publick Good ; yet as all new Deſigns at firſt uſually meet with Oppoſition and great Diſcouragements, rarely (if at all) pro-ving beneficial to the Firſt Adventurers, ſo hath this alſo incurr'd the ſame Fate hitherto, eſpe-cially from the Ignorant and Envious ; but the Undertakers do hope that all People will be Convinced, by time and experience, which removes Prejudice and Errors, and renders all New Undertakings Compleat ; for the Attainment of which good Ends, they have with great In-duſtry, much expence of time, and at a Chargeable Rate, made ſuch Alterations in their former Methods, as (they hope) will now give Univerſal ſatisfaction.   And whereas there has been much Noiſe about the pretended Delays and Miſcarriage of Letters going by the *Penny-Poſt,* which has riſen through the great Miſtake and Neglect of other People,   as the Undertakers can ſufficiently Evidence, by many Authentick Certificats which they have ready to produce, for the Juſtification of their due Performance in General, yet has there been ſo many Cauſleſs and Unjuſt Reflections caſt or ſo Uſeful an Undertaking, that they hold it highly Neceſſary to undeceive the World, by ſhewing ſome of the grounds from whence they ſpring, *viz.* . Some Men ſuppoſe, and confidently Alledge their Letters are Miſcarried, (or at leaſt Delayed,) becauſe they have not always an immediate Anſwer, when perhaps

A   the

But Dockwra continued with his idea and set up five sorting offices as well as between four and five hundred receiving houses. His messengers called every hour at the receiving houses to collect letters, take them to the sorting offices and deliver those already sorted. In some parts of the city there were as many as ten to twelve deliveries each day. Dockwra also invented his own stamps, some triangular, some heart-shaped, which told from which office the letters had been sent and the time of day as well.

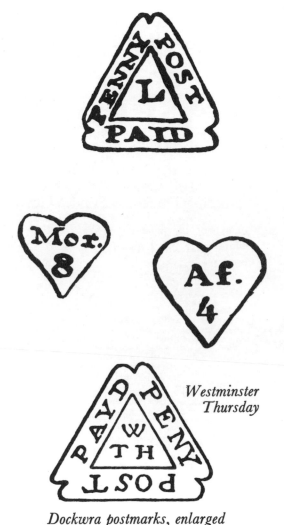

*Westminster
Thursday*

Dockwra postmarks, enlarged

The government did nothing about this private venture at first—perhaps they expected it to fail. However, when it was seen that the Penny Post was a good idea, the Duke of York, the King's brother, who enjoyed the profits made by the official Post Office (the system of "farming" was not then in use), took Dockwra to court. Dockwra, of course, lost the case. He had to pay a fine of £100 and his Penny Post was taken from him.

Because the Dockwra post was a success, the government took it over and ran it as an official post. Similar handstamps were used and they are known among collectors now as "Government Dockwras". When William and Mary came to the throne, Dockwra was better treated. In 1690 he was granted a yearly pension of £500, and in 1697 was made Comptroller of the Penny Post—his own post. But unfortunately he had enemies who accused him of not being honest and in 1700 he was dismissed.

The numbering of houses did not start until about 1767. In the Stuart period, to help those who could not read, picture signs were hung outside private houses much in the same way as they are hung outside inns and public houses today. Often coffee houses were used as places to which letters could be addressed, rather than to private houses. The owner of a coffee house would collect any letters addressed to his house from the Post Office, and hold them until the owners came in for cups of coffee. This was good for his trade, as well as being convenient for those expecting letters. "At the Pestell and Mortar", "At the Flying Horse", "At the Coffee Shop" are examples of the phrases used in old addresses.

Houses, inns and coffee houses had hanging signs instead of numbers. Below are photographs of two seventeenth-century letters showing how they were addressed. The one on the left has a Bishop Mark and the one on the right an original Dockwra stamp

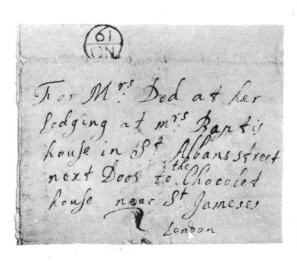

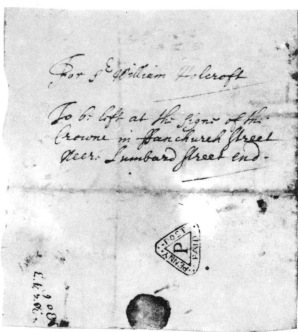

7 *POVEY AND WILLIAMSON*

In 1708 a man named Charles Povey thought up a scheme for a halfpenny post in the cities of London and Westminster and the borough of Southwark. He started his post in the next year but the Postmaster summoned him for running a private post and he was fined £100.

One idea of Povey's was kept by the Post Office after his halfpenny post was closed. He had used bellmen to walk round the streets to collect letters after the receiving offices were closed. They were paid twelve shillings a week and a penny for every letter collected.

Another man to start a penny post, this time in Edinburgh, was a man named Peter Williamson. Because of his early life and adventures he was sometimes called "Indian Peter".

When he was thirteen years old he was kidnapped in Aberdeen by some ruffians, who put him, along with fifty other children, on a boat bound for America, where they were to be sold as slaves.

Peter was bought by a farmer named Wilson

Peter wrote a diary, in which he tells how he was sold to a Scottish farmer named Wilson who had himself been sold as a slave years before. The farmer treated his new slave well and left him £150 and his best horse in his will.

Peter was seventeen years old when Mr. Wilson died, and for the next seven years he wandered about doing odd jobs. Then he married the daughter of a well-to-do planter. The planter gave his daughter and her husband a 200-acre farm and for a time all went well. But French settlers were stirring up trouble. They wanted to get the English out of North America, so they promised the Red Indians £15 for every English settler they killed.

Peter's home was attacked, his wife murdered and he himself was captured and made to work for the Indians. At times, he was tortured with burning wood when he did not please his captors.

At last he managed to escape, and he at once joined the British Army to fight against the French. He was wounded in the hand and sent back to England. On landing at Plymouth he was discharged from the army and given the sum of six shillings.

He decided to make his way back to his native Scotland. It was a long journey and he had very little money, so to make a living, he began exhibiting himself in Indian clothes complete with feathered head-dress, and uttering war cries. This is how he earned his nickname of "Indian Peter".

Peter Williamson in his Indian clothes

When he reached Aberdeen Peter Williamson tried to get his kidnappers punished, but those who were still alive had become powerful merchants. They turned him out of Aberdeen as a tramp and he set off for Edinburgh. Here he was luckier; judges listened to his story, and he was able to get money in compensation for what he had suffered. He opened up an inn which he called "Peter's Tavern", and it was here that he thought about starting a penny post in the city of Edinburgh.

This post started in about the year 1774. Peter's messengers, whom he called caddies, were given a uniform. For nineteen years this successful venture was allowed to carry on without interference from the G.P.O. and it was not until 1793 that the Williamson Post was taken over, but unlike Dockwra he was not arrested and fined. He was given a pension of £25 a year, and on this he lived quite happily until his death in 1799.

Towards the end of the seventeenth century, letter-carriers (or postmen) were being used in London, Edinburgh and Dublin. For many years these were the only cities where there was a free delivery of letters.

A letter-carrier of 1793

Before the Great Fire of 1666, the General Post Office stood near where Cannon Street station is now built. After the Fire it reopened in Lombard Street, where it remained until 1829. In that year it was transferred to St. Martin's-le-Grand. There were three separate departments in the old office: the *Inland Office* which dealt with all letters from the country, the *Foreign Office* which dealt with all foreign mail and the *Penny Post Office* which dealt with all local London letters.

Each office had its own staff of letter-carriers. These men, besides delivering the letters, had to collect the money due on them. Very few letters were paid for at the time of posting. In fact it was almost considered bad manners to do so.

The old General Post Office in Lombard Street, London, in about 1800

Not all letters were delivered. Some people preferred to collect their mail at the G.P.O. where "windowmen" sat at windows handing out letters and collecting the dues.

In other parts of the country, local postmasters were making money for themselves in a way which was illegal. They were charging an extra penny for delivering letters. Some postmasters, in many cases from kindness of heart, did deliver letters for nothing, but far more were charging the extra penny.

As years went by, the public began to object to the "delivery penny" as it became known. In 1774, a case was brought to the King's Bench Court and the judges ruled that the Post Office was bound to deliver letters free within the boundaries of each Post Town. This was a very important decision because it marks the beginning of the delivery service which we have today.

A windowman handing over a letter

8 THE CROSS POSTS

*A surveyor's wheel
of 1720*

A very important Post Office Act was passed in 1711. The old Tudor measurements of the roads were still being used, in spite of the fact that John Ogilvy, a map maker, had pointed out, in 1674, that many of them were incorrect. The new Act ordered the appointment of Road Surveyors to check all distances on the six post roads. Many errors were found.

Besides the General Post, two other unofficial posts were in existence at this time. They were known as "Bye" Posts and "Cross" Posts. A "bye letter" was one which did not have to pass from one post road to another, but could be collected and delivered by the postboy without his having to take it to London.

Cross posts were unofficial posts which had sprung up linking towns on different post roads thereby cutting down distance, time and cost. An early Cross Post had been started in 1696 between Bristol and Exeter. The postage cost had been reduced from 6d. to 2d.

But the Postmaster General could not check the extent of these posts. Some dishonest country postmasters overcharged the public, entering the correct charges in the returns which they made to London, and pocketing the overcharged amounts for themselves. Some of the postboys carried bye letters privately and made no returns at all. False robberies were reported in which it was said that the mail had been robbed and some postboys were even found to be working with the highwaymen.

It was because of these abuses that in 1715 the Postmaster General asked the Treasury to appoint six surveyors, or inspectors, one for each of the six post roads. The Treasury agreed. This system of Post Office Surveyors lasted until 1940, when the Second World War brought it to an end.

Ralph Allen, Postmaster of Bath, in 1754

The Cross Post system was improved by Ralph Allen who was the son of a Cornish innkeeper. His grandmother kept the post office in St. Columb, and Ralph, as a boy, often stayed with her and helped her to keep her books. In fact he was praised by a travelling inspector for the neatness of his figures.

In 1719 he was postmaster in Bath and he made up his mind to improve the running of the bye and cross posts. He offered the Postmaster General £6,000 per year if they would allow him to run these posts between Exeter and Chester and between Bristol and Oxford. His offer was quickly accepted as it was intended to close these posts in any case as they did not pay.

Allen was to receive all the money he made, and, of course, he had to stand the loss if he did not make the posts pay.

"The Post Office" (*from a painting by F. Goodall*)

But Ralph Allen did not fail. He appointed his own inspectors who worked with, not against, the official inspectors. Year by year the contract between the Post Office and himself was renewed. Year by year the Cross Post system increased, so that when Allen died in 1764 a rich man, there were cross posts all over the country.

9 THE MAIL COACH ERA

Another great change was the introduction of the Mail Coach. This idea was thought of by John Palmer, the son of a brewer who was born in Bath in 1742. It was during his visits to London that he noticed that the workings of the post were not always satisfactory.

A postboy of 1772

He thought it would be a good idea to use stage coaches instead of postboys to deliver the mail. These men took about three days to bring letters from Bristol to London. Merchants often complained and said they considered that fourteen or fifteen hours should be enough time for the journey.

John Palmer carefully thought out a scheme and, in 1782, he was able to meet William Pitt, Chancellor of the Exchequer, to talk over the matter. Pitt was interested and put the plan to the heads of the Post Office. These gentlemen did not like the idea at all and made many objections. These were collected and made into book form. Three large volumes were filled!

Much was made of the fact that Palmer was not connected with the Post Office. He should be told to mind his own business and not interfere. One gentleman named Hodgson said he considered the post to be "well regulated, carefully attended to, and not to be improved". He said further that the system was almost perfect and he and his friends could not see why the post should be the "swiftest conveyance in England".

John Palmer at the age of 17

In his reply, Palmer suggested that a trial was the only way to prove whether he was right, and William Pitt agreed with him. In 1784 a trial run that took place between Bristol and London was a complete success and the run was completed in sixteen hours.

The first coaches used were the ordinary heavy road coaches. Horses had to be changed every six miles.

With the improvement of the roads brought about by John McAdam and others, a new lighter coach was used. This was introduced by Charles Bonnor, who was Palmer's deputy. Soon these coaches reached an average speed of ten miles per hour and on some good roads as much as 20 m.p.h.

The original Bath Mail Coach of 1784

At first the coach builders supplied drivers and armed guards. This did not work well because the wrong type of man was employed. The Post Office later undertook to supply the guards who were allowed to carry firearms, which, it seems, they often used merely to make a noise. An Act of Parliament passed in 1790 stated that P.O. guards were not to fire except to defend themselves.

The wage of a guard was 13s. a week and 3s. was kept back for a uniform and a pension and sickness scheme. In addition he was always able to pick up tips from the passengers he guarded.

So, after 1799, when all the heavy coaches had been replaced by the newer and faster types, two coach services served the public. The first was the privately owned stage coach. The second service was supplied by the fast mail coach.

The privately owned stage coaches, which carried passengers and parcels, could also, with special permission, carry mail. They generally ran by day and were charged the heavy toll, or road tax, which was collected at the toll gates. Although they ran to timetables, no real attempt was made to keep to them. Drivers often waited for important passengers or for those who were known to tip well. Sometimes rival coaches raced each other along the roads with little thought for the comfort of the passengers. Accidents were far too frequent and in bad weather or in winter, coaches were withdrawn without notice.

A stage coach nearing a toll gate

The mail coaches had none of the highly coloured paint work and high-sounding names of the stage coaches, such as *Tally-Ho, Tantivy, Vivid,* and *Quicksilver.* They were all painted black and maroon, and each one carried the name of the route it was to travel. The four Royal Orders (Garter, Thistle, St. Patrick and Bath) were painted on the doors and upper panels. The "Mail" ran by night, with guards who were armed government servants. Travel was much safer and more satisfactory because of this. Attacks on the mail coaches were not nearly so common as on the stage coaches.

Passengers on mail coaches were pleased that they did not have to pay toll on the roads. The people who controlled the turnpike gates on the roads strongly objected to this special permission being granted to the Post Office. They said that the "Mails" took all the best traffic and paid nothing for the upkeep of the roads.

In 1836 there were 104 four-horsed mail coaches and a number of two-horsed ones for shorter journeys. Most of these started from London. It was considered one of the sights of old London to see the "Mail" leave every night from outside the General Post Office. The coaches, all cleaned and greased, were brought to various city inns where they were loaded with passengers and luggage. For example, the Bristol coach left from the *Swan with Two Necks* in Lad Lane, the Edinburgh coach from the *Bull and Mouth* in St. Martin's-le-Grand, and the Hull coach from the *Spread Eagle.*

The Royal Mail about to start from the G.P.O.

Just before 8 p.m. the coaches would be driven to the G.P.O. Here, among the noise of the busy streets, the coaches were lined up in the order in which they were to leave. One by one they were driven to the main door, where the guard received the leather bags containing the letters, which he carefully locked in the locker under his seat. Then, on a three-foot-long brass horn, he sounded the Post Horn Gallop, a way was cleared through the narrow streets and the coach was on its way.

The life of the mail coach service was short, because in 1830 mails began to be carried on the newly invented railway. The first railway service was between London and Manchester, and although horse-drawn coaches continued to be used for years in outlying parts such as Cornwall, the last mail coach departed from London in 1848.

The sorting office in the G.P.O., Lombard Street, in 1809

Not long ago, in the town of Chichester, there was discovered in the office of one of the local firms an old posting book. This book had been kept by the local postmaster, Mr. Fuller, and for this service he had charged the firm one guinea a year. On an average the firm at that time spent about £60 each year on postage.

At the end of 1839, after the entry for the 4th of December, a line was drawn across the page. Another line was drawn across after the entry for 9th January 1840.

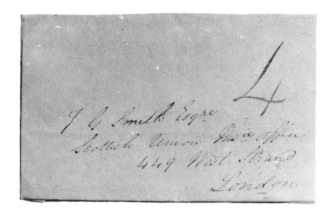

This letter travelled from Edinburgh to London for a charge of 4d. The amount of postage on this letter was impressed by a handstamp, not written by hand as was usual

During this short period £3 2s. 1d. was spent on postage, but only 10s. of this sum was spent during the last nine days. A grand new entry was made on 10th January. Seventy letters were posted on that day, but the cost was only 5s. 10d.

Can you guess why special new entries were made on the two dates mentioned, and why the firm held back some of the letters written between 1st January and 9th January?

The answer is that on 5th December 1839 and again on 10th January 1840, new postal rates were introduced. From 5th December 1839 to 9th January 1840 the postal rate on all letters to be posted and delivered in the United Kingdom was reduced to 4d. no matter what distance they had to travel. 10th January 1840 was a great day in the lives of a group of men, led by Rowland Hill. On that day all letters under half an ounce in weight could be sent to any place in the United Kingdom for a penny. This is the reason why the Chichester firm held back some of the letters which had been written between the 1st and the 9th of that month.

In 1837 Rowland Hill had published a pamphlet called "Post Office Reform". He was very concerned because so many people had found ways of cheating the Post Office. It had become a kind of game and some even boasted, quite openly, how they managed to do it. Postage could be paid when the letters were collected (pre-paid), or at the time of delivery. Most of the cheating was carried out when the letters were not paid for at the time of collecting.

Many stories are told about the methods used to avoid payment. Some people used the local carriers. Around Birmingham the carriers had set up a regular system, actually employing people to collect and deliver the letters.

POST OFFICE REGULATIONS.

On and after the 10th January, a Letter not exceeding **half an ounce in weight,** may be sent from any part of the United Kingdom, to any other part, for **One Penny,** if paid when posted, or for **Twopence** if paid when delivered.

THE SCALE OF RATES,

If paid when posted, is as follows, for all Letters, whether sent by the General or by any Local Post,

Not exceeding ½ Ounce . . . . One Penny.
Exceeding ½ Ounce, but not exceeding 1 Ounce . . Twopence.
Ditto   1 Ounce . . . . 2 Ounces Fourpence.
Ditto   2 Ounces . . . . 3 Ounces Sixpence.
and so on; an additional Two-pence for every additional Ounce. With but few exceptions, the WEIGHT is limited to Sixteen Ounces.

If not paid when posted, double the above Rates are charged on Inland Letters.

COLONIAL LETTERS.

If sent by Packet Twelve Times, if by Private Ship Eight Times, the above Rates.

FOREIGN LETTERS.

The Packet Rates which vary, will be seen at the Post Office. The Ship Rates are the same as the Ship Rates for Colonial Letters.

As regards Foreign and Colonial Letters, there is no limitation as to weight. All sent outwards, with a few exceptions, which may be learnt at the Post Office, must be paid when posted as heretofore.

Letters intended to go by Private Ship must be marked " *Ship Letter.*"

Some arrangements of minor importance, which are omitted in this Notice, may be seen in that placarded at the Post Office.

No Articles should be transmitted by Post, which are liable to *injury,* by being stamped, or by being crushed in the Bags.

It is particularly requested that all Letters may be *fully* and *legibly addressed,* and *posted as early* as convenient.

January 7th, 1840.

By Authority:—J. Hartnell, London.

The new Post Office regulations for 10th January 1840

Newspapers could be sent free through the post providing no messages had been written on them and people tried many ways of making use of these.

Sorting newspapers in the G.P.O., 1845

Milk was often used as a kind of invisible ink. A message written with it would show up when heated. By pricking out or dotting letters in newspapers, messages could be made up. A newspaper was sometimes used to inform a letter writer that his letter had been received. He would write "Send me an old newspaper, and I will know that you have received my letter".

Sometimes a letter was marked with some secret sign or the address was written in a certain way so that the person receiving it could see at a glance that all was well with the sender and could refuse the letter and so avoid the payment.

Some privileged persons, such as Members of Parliament, were allowed to send their letters free. All such a person had to do was to sign his name in the bottom right corner and the letter would be stamped "Free". It had become quite a profitable business for some dishonest Members to sell these "Free Franks" as they were called.

The message on this letter of 1839 reads: "Not a frank to be got, but hopes held out of a penny post in January"

Rowland Hill

The Committee set up in 1837 to look into the matter of Postal Reform sat in Bruce Castle, Tottenham. Rowland Hill told this committee that his idea was to persuade people to pay the postage at the time of posting. He said that if a scheme could be worked out by which everybody paid the same amount, the work inside the Post Office would be greatly reduced.

As the law then stood, each letter which came into the Post Office had to be treated by itself and the charge was fixed according to the distance it had to travel, its weight and whether it was made up of one or more sheets of paper. All this work kept a large number of men busy who could be doing other work.

Of course, there were some who did not agree with Rowland Hill. It seemed sensible, they said, that a letter sent from London to Edinburgh should cost more than one sent from London to Guildford in Surrey. Hill argued that if the postage were made much cheaper and the same all over the country, more people would write letters, more men would be employed and more money would flow into the Treasury.

"Bagging" letters for the large towns

Many thought that this scheme could not possibly work. They believed that the Post Office would lose so much money that the Government would have to raise taxes on other things. Some businessmen were worried at the thought of more than one delivery of letters a day. This was bound to happen if, as Hill hoped, more letters were to be written. They were used to getting all their letters first thing in the morning. A second delivery, and perhaps a third, would upset all their office arrangements, and they did not see why they should be expected to alter them.

Gradually Hill managed to persuade people that he was right. But how was he to be sure that the letters had been paid for when they were posted?

An entry for the Treasury Competition

The idea of a "sticky label" was suggested to him by a Mr. Charles Knight. Accordingly, a competition, known as the Treasury Competition, was published in *The Times* newspaper on 6th September 1839. People were asked to send in designs which would be convenient, cheap to produce and difficult to forge. £200 was to be paid to the winner and £100 to the next best.

Many designs were sent in and four were selected, but in the end none of these designs was used.

38

Instead, Mr. Cole, one of Rowland Hill's strongest supporters, went to a famous artist, William Mulready, R.A., and asked him to produce a design for envelopes and wrappers which could be sold to the public. So far envelopes were not generally used for letters, the sheet of paper was simply folded up and sealed with wax, and the address was written on the outside.

In the meantime an Act of Parliament had been passed setting up a Uniform Post. There was to be a short period of a Uniform Fourpenny Post from 5th December 1839 to 10th January 1840. After that date the Uniform Penny Post was to come into operation. During the Fourpenny period the charge mark on the letters was to be a handwritten 4, but in fact some twenty-five towns had metal handstamps made. It was intended that sticky labels were to be used when the Uniform Penny Post started, but unfortunately there had been delays over choosing the design and over getting the sheets of labels gummed. The result was that they were not ready in time.

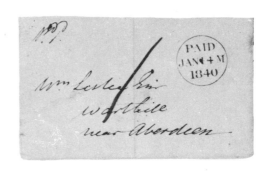

The front and back of a letter posted on 14th January 1840. Notice the handwritten 1 across the address which was put on in red by the postmaster. The sender has written "Pd. 1d." in the top left hand corner

Below are some penny post markings from different towns. Many towns made their own and designs varied. Notice the back-to-front Ns on the middle stamp

Handstamps of Aberystwyth and Bradford

For a time, therefore, handstamps had to be used; saying usually "1d. Paid". Over 350 towns had handstamps of different designs, and these were still used up to 1853, when the use of labels became compulsory. As these handstamps were made by local craftsmen some curious mistakes occur. Letters were sometimes cut the wrong way round.

*The Wyon Medal
used for the
engraving of the
Penny Black*

*The Penny Black
issued 6th May
1840*

The design eventually chosen for the labels, or stamps as we now call them, was that of Queen Victoria's head as used on the Wyon medal. This had been designed by William Wyon, the chief designer to the Royal Mint, to commemorate the visit of the Queen to the City of London in 1839.

The design was engraved on to a steel plate by Charles and Frederick Heath (father and son), and was printed in sheets of 240. The sheet was made up of twenty rows, each with twelve labels, and each label had different corner letters, the first row beginning A-A and ending A-L and the last row beginning T-A and ending T-L.

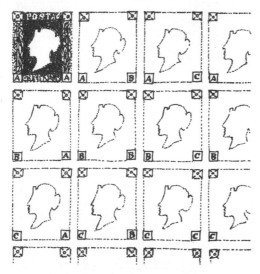

The beginning of the first, second and third rows of a large sheet of stamps. Notice how the stamps are lettered in the bottom corners, the left hand corner indicating the row and the right hand corner the position of the stamp in the row

The public had to be told where to stick and how to stick the labels. The inscription on the stamp edging gave this information; "Price 1d. per label; 1s. per row of 12; £1 per sheet. Place the label ABOVE the address and towards the RIGHT HAND SIDE of the letter. In wetting the Back be careful not to remove the Cement." (Today we use the word "gum" instead of "cement".)

Circulars were sent to the postmasters informing them that the sale of the new labels (1d. black for letters of half an ounce and 2d. blue for letters over that weight but under one ounce) was to commence on 6th May 1840. A specimen of each label was given.

Various types of locally cut Maltese crosses

Twopenny Blue of 1841 cancelled with a Maltese cross

On each circular, too, instruction was given as to the method of cancelling. A handstamp shaped like a Maltese cross was provided which was to be pressed into a pad of prepared red ink and EACH label was to be cancelled by one strike. Sometimes postmasters lost their original handstamps and had replacements made locally. These differed in details from the originals, and collectors today search for letters and stamps cancelled by these local Maltese crosses.

On the 6th of May the public were to be able to buy the new Mulready envelopes and wrappers, but for some reason people did not like the design. Other artists soon began to draw other designs to make fun of the Mulready design. These envelopes are known as the "Mulready caricatures". The author has a used Mulready posted on the 28th May 1840, only twenty-two days after the wrappers were on sale to the public. On this wrapper the writer has written, "Your envelope was the first of these I saw for several days". He also called attention to another difficulty—"I cannot make the labels adhere —can you?"

Mulready envelope

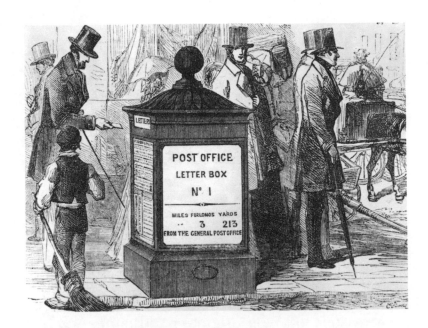

London's first pillar box, 1855. It was situated at the corner of Fleet Street and Farringdon Street

The labels, or stamps as we shall now call them, were imperforate. This means that there were no rows of small holes between the stamps as we have today. It was some eleven years later that a man named Henry Archer invented a perforating machine. Until then all the stamps had to be cut round with scissors. To save themselves trouble, the Post Office clerks usually began their day by cutting the sheets of Blacks and Blues into strips of twelve. This is the reason that today it is much more common to find strips of these stamps than to find blocks (joined stamps from two or more rows). There were many difficulties to be overcome in the early days of perforating stamps as can be seen in the illustration below.

A stamp which shows the difficulties of perforating

During the eleven months of the life of the Penny Black, over 68 million were printed, and of that number it is estimated that about 6 million have survived. Collectors today like to have "Blacks" in their collections, not because they are rare (which they are not) but because they were the first stamps issued anywhere in the world.

Other countries soon followed Great Britain's lead, Brazil and Switzerland being two of the earliest. As the number of stamp-issuing countries grew, so did the number of people who began to collect stamps.

By 1856 a number of these stamp collectors used to meet in London and dealers soon began to deal in rare stamps and many interesting stories are told of "finds".

A young man named Gibbons began a stamp dealer's business in Plymouth. One morning in 1863 two sailors called and asked if he bought stamps. He told them he did.

The next day they returned with a kit-bag full, which they said they had won in a raffle in Cape Town whilst on shore leave. One of the sailors tipped the contents on to a table. The bag contained thousands and thousands of the triangular stamps then used in Cape Colony. Needless to say the dealer bought the lot and made a good profit.

A Cape triangular shilling stamp issued in 1858

The second story concerns a friend of the author. One day in September 1949 he was offered a large box full of Great Britain Penny Reds. This carton contained thousands of this very common stamp, which is the same design as the Penny Black but was printed in red so that it could be cancelled in black.

Now although this stamp is so common, there are one or two printing mistakes which are very difficult to find.

Stamp showing the
B-(A) blank

One of the most famous of these mistakes is known as the B-A blank. The little letters in the corners of these stamps were punched in by hand. Somehow the workman punching the letters on the printing plate forgot to punch the letter A in the bottom right corner of the first stamp of the B row. Less than twenty copies are known to exist so the chance of finding another is very slight. However, late one night, having decided to search through just one more pile, my friend discovered another copy of this valuable rarity. This made months of searching worth while.

Anyone who is interested in these fascinating stories of early stamps can find them in books in some of the public libraries, but this last story will not be found, because it has never before been printed.

II SHIP LETTERS

As soon as ships began to be used for trading, it became necessary for merchants of different countries to write letters to one another. It was part of the duties of ships' masters to carry these letters and to see that they were delivered. This was, however, a private service, and letters so carried were not classed as Ship Letters until 1657. In that year an Act of Parliament stated that all letters brought into this country were to be posted in the ordinary way and were to be charged as ordinary mail. No official payment was made at first to the ships' masters, but later they were granted a payment of one penny a letter handed in at the port of arrival.

Ship's captain accepting a letter

The passing of this Act in 1657 and again in 1660 did not prevent the smuggling of private letters into the country. Most Ship Letters in the seventeenth century came into the Port of London and it became a trick of the masters to drop all letters addressed to London in the London Penny Post, thereby saving on postage. For example, a letter from Marseilles to London would be charged at the foreign rate of a shilling, but if it could be smuggled into the Penny Post, 11d. would be saved. In 1696 the Postmasters General tried to stop this by appointing two officers to receive letters and packets from all "masters of ships and vessels, mariners and passengers as shall be by them hereafter brought in any ships or vessels into the Port of London".

Ships used by the Government to carry letters were called *Packets*. In 1711 an Act was passed which made it illegal to send letters by private ships to places which were visited by Government Packets. To countries not served by Packets, letters could be sent by private ship and the master could charge as he wished.

A Post Office Packet of the early nineteenth century

In those days the coffee houses were the popular meeting houses where men gathered together to talk and discuss the business of the day. Newspapers were very dear and coffee house keepers found that a good way of attracting customers was to display the latest papers for them to read.

Some of the more important coffee houses collected letters to be sent by private ship. Ship owners usually charged 2d. a letter, and as, in many cases, this was cheaper than the Government charge, private ships continued to take letters on routes where there were official Packets.

Letters written from abroad were often addressed to coffee houses—"At the coffee house in St. James's" or "At the coffee house in the Strand". This meant that people expecting letters would call at the coffee houses to collect them.

Letters were delivered to coffee houses

To try to stop this use of private ships, a Ship Letter Office was opened in 1796. It was found that by making ships' captains hand over the mail they were carrying to the Post Office before "breaking bulk" (unloading cargoes), it was fairly easy to control letters coming into the country.

Every person who received a ship letter had to pay 4d. more than the cost of the ordinary postage charged on the letter from the port of arrival to his home. For example, if a letter had been landed at Portsmouth and was to be sent on to Guildford, near London, the charge to the receiver would be 9d.—4d. for the ship letter charge and 5d. for sending it from Portsmouth to Guildford at the inland rate. The master of the ship received 2d. for every letter which he handed over to the Post Office.

But it was much more difficult to keep watch on the letters going out of the country. The Post Office officials tried to get the coffee house keepers to work for them but the plan failed and it became known that eighteen times more letters left this country by private ship than came in.

Incoming letters were marked "Ship Letter" with the name of the port of arrival.

Portsmouth Ship Letter

Practically every village or town with a harbour large enough to hold a vessel was given a Ship Letter handstamp. There are many different designs and some are very difficult to find.

In the days of sail, vessels were often driven off course by wind or storm and since captains did not wish to lose the letters which they carried, they often put in at the first British port they came to. There they handed over the letters to the Post Office man and received their payment (2d. for each letter carried). What happened to the letters after that was no concern of theirs. In times of war, captains often put in at small ports to avoid enemy ships.

When postage became cheaper the smuggling of letters died out and today the Post Office has control over all letters going out or coming into this country.

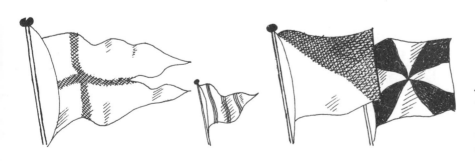

Some of the flags flown by the Falmouth Post Office Packet. Each commander had his own flag

12 SOME SPECIAL SERVICES OF THE POST OFFICE

From time to time the Post Office started special services and charged special rates of postage for them. Some have died out, but others have survived and are still being used to this day.

Express Services

From early times very urgent and important letters could be sent by using special messengers. If, in 1751, a person wanted to send a letter by a Post Office messenger to Edinburgh, he had to obtain special permission from the Post Office in London. The charge was £5 1s. Obviously, only the very rich could afford to use this service and many private express companies were started, but it was not until 1891 that the G.P.O. began a public service. The messenger charge was 2d. for the first mile, 3d. for the second mile and a shilling for each other mile where no public transport could be obtained. It was still a costly business to send a letter by express service.

A telegraph messenger of 1904

In 1895 living creatures and liquids could be sent by the express. This led to an amusing happening in 1909. Women were demanding the vote and those who took an active part were called suffragettes. The Prime Minister, Mr. Asquith, refused to meet these women at No. 10 Downing Street, so two of them were posted "express" to him. The police could not stop them because they must not "intercept postal packets in transmission by post".

When the two "live packets" arrived at No. 10 the butler refused to take them in and they were returned as "dead letters" to the person who sent them. (A "dead" letter is one sent by post which is unclaimed or undelivered.)

Today there are three kinds of Express Delivery. The first is when the packet is taken all the way by a Post Office messenger; the second when a packet is posted in the ordinary way and the messenger delivers it from the receiving office; and the third is by Railex. In this case the packet is taken to a railway station by the messenger, sent by train and then may or may not be delivered by messenger at the end of the journey.

Parcel Post

The first parcel post in this country was begun by Dockwra in 1680, but this was for London only. It was not until 1st August 1883 that a parcel post for all the country was started. Up to that time parcels had been carried by carriers or private companies. Today no parcel heavier than 22 lb. can be sent through the post. In 1967 the charge was 2s. 6d. for the lightest parcel and 10s. 6d. for the heaviest, but rates are liable to change at any time.

Railway Letters

Before 1st February 1891 letters could not be sent by railway unless they were tied up with string. Then they were termed "parcels".

After this date the G.P.O. agreed that the railways could carry letters providing that each was stamped with a penny stamp and did not weigh more than one ounce. This weight was later raised to four ounces. Twopence was to be paid to the company on each letter handed in, and many companies issued their own stamps for this purpose. They were, by arrangement, to be green in colour.

Registration

Dockwra's Penny Post recorded details of all letters accepted and made payment if any were lost. This was a form of registration, although it relied largely on the goodwill of the owner. It was not until 1787 that official

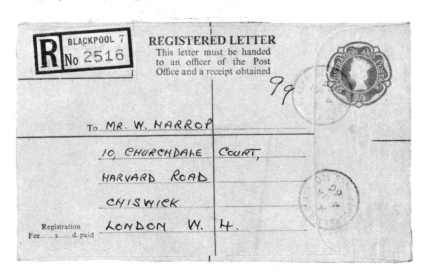

A registered letter

registration was begun, and then it was only on foreign letters. The fee charged was very heavy—one guinea—so the service was not much used.

The registration of inland letters (letters not leaving the country of origin) was introduced in 1841. The fee was one shilling but the rates have often changed since then. Today the lowest registration fee is 3s. for which the G.P.O. will cover loss up to £100. By paying larger fees, larger amounts can be insured.

13 AIR MAILS

Balloons were the first aerial machines used to carry mail. An attempt was made to get messages by balloon to Sir John Franklin who was lost in the Polar regions in 1847. Needless to say this hopeless venture failed. However, messages were successfully carried by balloon from the besieged city of Paris during the Franco-Prussian war of 1870.

A newspaper, the *Daily Graphic*, arranged a "Balloon Expedition" in October 1907. Special cards were carried showing a balloon over London bearing the words: "A message from mid-air".

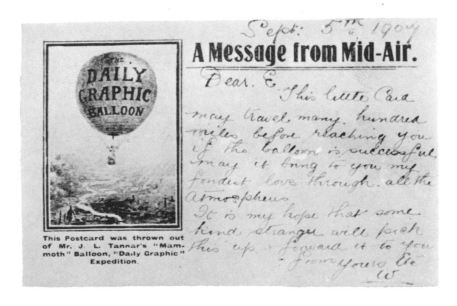

Balloon card of 1907

The first aeroplane mail flight was made on 10th August 1919. Letters were to be carried from Blackpool to Southport but owing to bad weather the machine, piloted by Graham White, could fly only seven miles.

Many other private air mail flights took place during the next twenty years, but the first air mail experiment in which the G.P.O. was interested took place in 1911.

Early aeroplane as piloted by Graham White

In that year King George V and Queen Mary were crowned and in September a number of flights, carrying special cards, took place between London and Windsor. These cards (and some envelopes) were cancelled with a special postmark "First United Kingdom—Aerial Post".

The first organised postal air service began between London and Paris in 1919. The charge for sending a letter was 2s. 6d. an ounce. People did not like to trust their letters to this new-fangled method nor did they like the heavy charge. Even when this dropped to 2d. an ounce the service did not become a real success.

Letter carried by Railway Air Services, 1934

However, as aeroplanes became more reliable and regular air routes were established, air mail services became more popular. From 1925 onwards they had begun to extend all over the world. In 1929 a London to India service was set up; a route to Singapore followed in 1933, and was extended to Darwin, Australia, in 1934.

Then followed the Empire Mail Scheme in 1935. This was put into operation in three stages. On 29th June 1937, the East and South Africa service was started; on 23rd February 1938 the second stage added main line service to India and Malaya; and the final extension from 28th July 1938 included Hong Kong and Australia. These "main line" routes were fed by local services. The saving of time was an important factor. The sea time to Bombay was 14 days while the air time was $2\frac{1}{2}$ days; the times to Cape Town were 14 days by sea and 4 days by air; the times to Sydney were 32 days by sea and 7 days by air.

In the meantime private companies had started internal air services. A London to Plymouth service began in 1933, as did a "West Country Air Service", and in 1934 came a Plymouth and Isle of Wight service. The outbreak of the Second World War in 1939 brought an end to air mail experiments, but after the war better and faster air services were started, so that today, with the help of other countries, all the world can be linked by air mail.

Loading the mail from a P.O. van on to aircraft at Nutt's Corner, Belfast

Trafalgar Square Branch Office, London. This post office is open day and night

14 THE POST OFFICE TODAY

The Postman's Uniform

One of the most familiar uniforms to be seen in our streets today is that of the postman. We all know his dark suit with its scarlet piping and his "pillar box" red bicycle or van. Pillar boxes and telephone kiosks in Britain are usually in this same brilliant colour although in some parts of the Lake District of England green is being used. It is said that the red spoils the natural beauty of the countryside.

The first mention of a special dress for letter-carriers in Britain comes from Aberdeen where, in 1590, these men wore blue suits with badges on the sleeves. The next mention of uniform was made in 1728 when the only distinguishing mark was a "brass ticket upon the visible part of his clothing, with the King's arms on the same". In 1784 mail coach guards and drivers were all given uniforms.

The postman today

The first real uniform issued was that given to the London letter-carriers of the General Post in 1793. It consisted of a gold banded beaver hat, a scarlet coat with blue lapels, and a blue cloth waistcoat with brass buttons. On these buttons was shown the wearer's post office number. The man had to provide his own trousers and boots. In 1837 a similar uniform, with a blue coat instead of red, was issued to each London District letter-carrier.

Quite a change took place in 1854 when all the letter-carriers in London were issued with waterproof capes, frock coats, trousers, caps instead of beaver hats and number badges on collars. Next year all appeared in scarlet coats and grey trousers.

Before 1860 only the London letter-carriers had been given uniforms, but in that year a general issue was made to all post offices whose letter-carriers earned sufficient money. Apparently country letter-carriers, who did not carry many letters but who often had long distances to walk, were not given uniforms.

In 1870 a telegraph service began and the boy messengers were given uniforms at once. Two years later full uniform was granted to all country letter-carriers. The name "letter-carrier" was dropped in 1884 and the word "postman" was used instead.

London General
Letter-Carrier
1793–1855

London District
Letter-Carrier
1837–1855

Letter-
Carrier
1862

Boy Messenger
1904

Provincial postman
1908

The "Hen and Chickens" centre cycle

At first letter-carriers either walked or used horses to deliver the mail, but in 1880 a tricycle post was started in Coventry. This was not a success. A Horsham architect planned a "centre cycle" which became nicknamed the "Hen and Chickens". One of these rather clumsy machines can be seen in the G.P.O. Headquarters building in London. This centre cycle was soon given up and ordinary bicycles were used instead. Motor vans were first used in 1919.

The Journey of a Letter

The Post Office today has many services to offer the public, but as the first of these was the carrying of letters, let us consider what happens to a letter written today. First it is posted in a pillar box. The first of these was used in Guernsey in 1852. The time of collecting is shown on the box and this will be changed when the postman collects the letters. Our letter is now on its way to the sorting office.

Here all the collecting bags are emptied and a first sorting begins. Ordinary sized letters are separated from newspapers, packets and long letters. The letters are then placed the right way round.

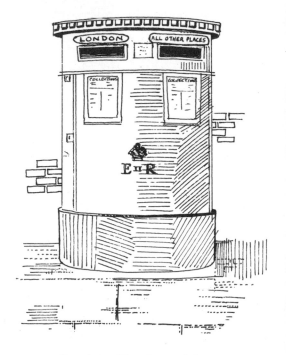

London pillar box with two mouths

The sorter looks to see that all the stamps are placed in the correct place, the right-hand top corner of the envelope. All letters which are not stamped or have stamps in the wrong places are put to one side. These have to be postmarked by hand, whereas all the others pass into a postmarking machine which can deal with about 800 letters a minute.

When all the letters are postmarked they are then sorted in sorting frames. These frames consist of forty-eight boxes, or pigeon holes, arranged in six rows of eight. Each box is labelled. Large counties have a box each; so have important cities. Smaller counties are grouped together into groups called "roads". There is a box for local mail and one for overseas mail. This first sorting is called Outward Primary sorting.

When this is finished the sorters collect together the contents of the boxes. The letters are then sorted into the Outward Secondary sorting frames, where they are sorted into large towns and post towns. A post town is one which serves a large country area in which are smaller towns and villages. So when the mail arrives at such a town it has to be sorted again. All this shows how important it is for us to address our letters correctly and clearly. Not long ago, a shopkeeper living in the town of Kingston-on-Thames sent a bill to a person living two or three roads away. The writer just addressed the envelope to Kingston and put it into the letter box. He was very surprised to have the letter returned to him some months later, with "Not known in Kingston, Ontario" and "Not known in Kingston, Jamaica" stamped on it. There was also a pencilled note "Try Kingston-on-Thames, England". The letter, badly addressed, had been sorted into the overseas box by accident.

A wonderful machine has now been invented which can do all this sorting work by electricity. The first of these machines was installed in the Southampton Post Office. All the mail to be sorted is tipped on to a moving belt or segregator. Parcels, packages and letters of all shapes and sizes move along into the automatic sorter. Here the letters are sorted from the more bulky packages.

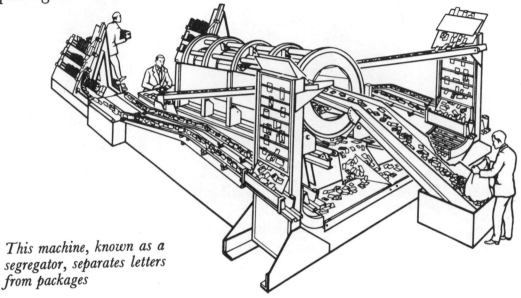

This machine, known as a segregator, separates letters from packages

Letters are fed into small moving tracks which hold them upright. Bulky packages cannot get on to these tracks and are therefore left behind. Letters of all sizes move along this first track which suddenly divides into two tracks, one for small letters and the other for larger ones. Any envelope which is too large to run on to the smaller track is rejected. It continues its journey on the large track.

The letters on these tracks are not all the right way round. Some are upside down and some back to front. Another part of this wonderful machine, the Automatic Letter Facer, called ALF for short, turns all the letters the correct way round with the stamps in the top right corners. ALF deals with about 300 letters each minute.

The letters go on to the postmarking section and finally to the letter sorting machine. This machine has 144 pigeon holes instead of 48 as in a hand sorting frame. Before each letter reaches the automatic sorter it drops down, for a moment, behind a glass screen. A sorter with a machine which looks something like a typewriter, sits in front of this screen. He looks at the

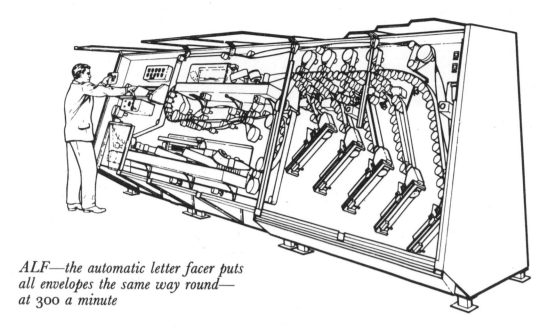

ALF—the automatic letter facer puts all envelopes the same way round— at 300 a minute

address on each letter and taps a code message. This code changes for each different town.

Away goes the letter on its journey. It travels along towards the sorting frame as though it knows where to go. When it reaches the box labelled for it, it leaves the track and comes to rest. About two letters every second are sorted on this machine.

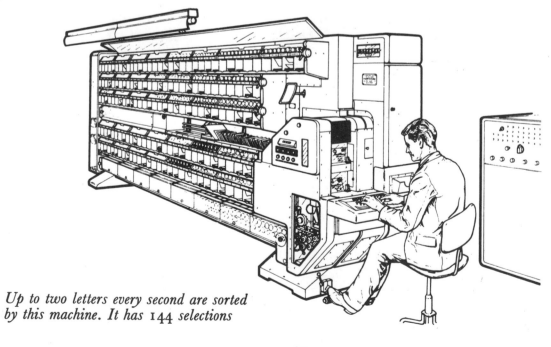

Up to two letters every second are sorted by this machine. It has 144 selections

Most of the inland mail which has any distance to travel goes by train. The sorted mail is taken to the railway station in G.P.O. vans where it is loaded into the guard's van of the train. The guard is in charge of it until it reaches the end of its journey where it will be collected by officials of the Post Office.

Inside a sorting coach on the T.P.O. Down

Some trains (more than seventy) include special vans in which unsorted mail can be sorted. Such a van is called a Travelling Post Office or T.P.O. The first one ran in 1838 between London and Preston. There are four trains, however, which are made up entirely of post office vans. The Down Special runs between Euston and Aberdeen, a distance of 540 miles; the Up Special runs between Aberdeen and London; T.P.O. Down runs between Paddington and Penzance and the T.P.O. Up between Penzance and Paddington.

Sorters on these trains get to work immediately the unsorted mail is loaded because more will be taken on during the journey and the sorted mail will be despatched. A great deal of this will be done while the train is moving at speed. Despatching arms are swung out from the side of the train. Leather bags which contain the sorted mail are fastened to these arms. By the side of the track are receiving nets which catch the mail bags from the despatching arms. When the train has to pick up mail to be sorted, its own nets pick up from despatching standards built along by the side of the track.

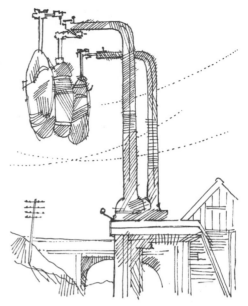

Despatching arms by the side of the railway track

At the Post Office Counter

The counter clerk helps a customer

The Post Office clerk of today has to do much more varied work than the clerk of a hundred years ago. He has to sell postage stamps of all values, postal orders, money orders, insurance stamps and registered envelopes. He has to know how to weigh and charge parcels and has to be able to quote the foreign postal rates. Of course he has books to refer to when necessary but he cannot always be looking up facts in a book when there is a queue of customers waiting to be served. He has to know how to check and charge for telegrams. He has to pay out Old Age pensions, war pensions, widows' pensions and family allowances.

The clerk also has to know what to do when customers ask for wireless or television licences, for dog, car or gun licences. He has to know how to handle Post Office Savings books, and the difference between "registration", "recorded delivery" and "certificate of posting". *Registration* is a kind of insurance—for a fee of 3s. the contents of a letter or parcel can be insured against loss providing that the value is less than £100. Threepence is added for each extra £100 value that is to be registered. A parcel valued at £400 would, therefore, have to be registered for 3s. and three extra threepences —3s. 9d. in all.

P 2297 G

D 682056

CERTIFICATE OF POSTING
FOR RECORDED DELIVERY

Enter below in ink or indelible pencil the name and
address as written on the letter or packet.

Name..

Address ....

....

→ **Instructions and Conditions of**
Acceptance see over   51 - 9792 C.P. LTD. 4/64

Date Stamp

Accepting
Officer's
Initials.................

D 682056 Recorded Delivery

You fill in a form like this if you wish to send a letter by recorded delivery. The stamp on the right of the form is torn off and stuck on the letter

By paying an extra ninepence anyone can send a letter *recorded delivery*. This means that the delivering of the letter is noted and that the sender can check this if he wants to. He cannot claim any money if the letter is lost.

Certificate of Posting is a certificate which states that a parcel has been handed in for posting. It is not a form of insurance and no money can be claimed from the Post Office if the parcel is lost.

There are many more things which a postal clerk has to know. These are all in a large book of nearly 500 pages which is called the *Post Office Guide*. This is re-issued every year and often alterations have to be made because the Postmaster General may have to make changes before a new "Guide" is sent out.

An old lady once asked a young postal clerk, "How do I post a pound of butter?" He found the answer in the "Guide" and passed the information on to the old lady. Many more awkward questions are asked every day and with the help of this important book the official answers can be given without much trouble.

Telephones

The U.S.A. section of the International Telephone Exchange

Nearly all the telephones in Great Britain belong to the G.P.O. This was not always so. In the middle of the nineteenth century private companies started a telephone service, but there were so many difficulties that the Post Office took over all the services in Britain (with the exception of Hull, Portsmouth and the Channel Islands) on 1st January 1912. Portsmouth was taken over soon after, but Hull and the Channel Islands still operate their own services.

The modern Post Office of Great Britain is rightly proud of its history, but it is always looking forward, trying to make its existing services to the public more efficient, and seeking new methods by which they may be improved.

More books for you to read

THE PENNY POST 1680–1918 by Frank Staff (Lutterworth)
FUN WITH STAMPS by Dianne Doubtfire and Kay Horowicz (Hutchinson)
MORE FUN WITH STAMPS by Dianne Doubtfire and Kay Horowicz (Hutchinson)
THE POSTMAN by F. Heathcote Briant (Ward Lock)
FROM PILLAR TO POST by L. Zilliacus (Heinemann)
HERE COMES THE POST by Boswell Taylor (University of London Press)

The G.P.O. has various books, leaflets and posters for schools which they will supply to teachers. Perhaps your teacher would like to apply to the Head Postmaster or Telephone Manager of your area for some of these.

Places to visit

An interesting museum to visit when in London is The National Postal Museum at 63 King Edward Street, E.C.1. This is open Mondays to Fridays from 10.30 a.m. to 4.30 p.m.

INDEX